THE BONE THAT SWALLOWED A MAN

Poems

Mark Vanner

Copyright © 2024 Mark Vanner

All rights reserved. No part of this publication may be reproduced, distributed, or transmitted in any form or by any means, including photocopying, recording, or other electronic or mechanical methods, without the prior written permission of the publisher, except in the case of brief quotations embodied in critical reviews and certain other non-commercial uses permitted by copyright law.

Front cover image/ interior design by:
ANXIETY DRIVEN GRAPHICS

ISBN: 9798328280112

AP

Table of Contents

8 *Introduction*

14 *Kathy's Dream*

17 *The Magician*

19 *Future Appliances*

21 *Scarecrow*

23 *You're Welcome*

26 *Dr. Freud*

28 *The Letter*

31 *Colony*

32 *Dumber*

35 *Statues*

37 *A Discourse In Cultural Heritage*

39 *In This Game We Are Playing*

40 *Apology*

43 *Tattoo*

45 *Return To Babel*

47 *Postcoital*

48 *TV Made Us Fat But Look At Us Now*

50 *Horseplay*

53 *Proper Gangsta*

54 *Vaba Banga*

56 *Spiritualist Night At The Old Bull Inn*

57 *Planet Woman*

58 *Strange Fish*

60 *A Musical Theatre Piece Based On The Story Of The Windrush Generation And Played Exclusively By White, Upper-Class Actors*

61 *Yellow Submarine*

63 *Jackpot*

65 *Every Crack Represents A Life I Have Saved*

67 *The Drill*

68 *The Dream Shop*

70 *A Message To Future Cat Generations*

71 *A Zero-Tolerance Approach*

73 *Buddha On A Bicycle*

75 *Discombobulation*

77 *An Existential Crisis*

79 *The Art Gallery*

80 *Procession*

82 *Post Historic Shame*

84 *Blood Axe Books*

86 *Acknowledgments*

About The Author

INTRODUCTION

I came to learn about Mark Vanner through his visual art. He's a painter, and his stark work is eye-catching – stunning, even. It's redolent of painters I admire – Francis Bacon leaps immediately to mind -- if not exactly in style, then in content. But Mark's work is unique and shouldn't really be compared to anyone else. What I love most about it is that it captures our horror at existence itself, not to mention that it's deliciously mysterious and executed with the skill of a great craftsman. I'm honored to own a couple of his paintings, and wish I owned more.

Mark and I subsequently became unlikely across-the-pond friends – he's somewhere in Gloucestershire, and I'm not far from the Lincoln Tunnel, and through our conversations, I learned that he's not only a painter but a writer as well. Well, this was of particular interest to me since we're both multidisciplinary, or Renaissance men, or whatever our type is called nowadays. The point is that neither of us can seem to resist the impulse to stray beyond where we're supposed to be quartered. It also means we have lots in common, and issues to negotiate: how to balance all the effort that goes into painting, and writing, and composing, how those disciplines cross-pollinate, how you go about executing your work, and so on. There is always much to talk about when the subjects we're wrestling with are so big.

Then Mark's poems fell into my hands. I was immediately intrigued by them, and quite surprised in many ways. They were more or less the equivalent in verse of his paintings, which I should have expected. Brilliantly crafted, subtle, and startlingly original, they penetrate to the core of the human experience and its mystery, and always keep you more than a little off balance -- always the goal of the writer who wants the intelligent reader to keep pushing forward.

If you have this collection in your hands, count yourself very lucky. You are about to meet Mark Vanner. You are about to enter his world through his poems. And they are fascinating. You won't be disappointed. For him it's just the start in the world of letters, but I expect we will be hearing from him for a long time to come.

Mark SaFranko, October 2023

*The Bone
That Swallowed
A Man*

If they give you ruled paper, write the other way.

— Juan Ramón Jiménez

Kathy's Dream

I spent weeks visiting a therapist;
Trying to process what was happening to me -
what was happening to Kathy -
It all seemed so impossible.
Take your time, the Therapist said,
as I stared at the giant,
smudge-like painting on the wall.
For the past forty years, I said,
I believed I was in control of my life.
Thought I was the master of my own destiny.
The captain of my own vessel.
Then I discovered I was just a figment of Kathy's dream.
The Therapist handed me a box of tissues.
How? She said.
I looked across at Kathy
who was fiddling with a braid
of her cherry-blonde hair
and then back to the Therapist
whose head had transformed into a gigantic
grey squirrel.
For a long time, I said. *I found it strange*
that time didn't move in any orderly direction
and that the surrounding scenery was constantly

shifting. Then I realised,
I couldn't remember a moment in my life
when Kathy wasn't with me.
Now everything seems...
So meaningless.
It's okay, squawked the Therapist
from behind an orange beak.
We've all been where you are now.
Understanding that our lives are utterly pointless
is the first step to acceptance.
But what will happen, I asked,
when Kathy stops dreaming of me?
I suppose it'll be like falling asleep and never waking up,
the Therapist said.
But...
Yes? She said.
I'm scared, I said.
We all are, she said.
I gazed at the painting on the wall
for what seemed like an inordinately long time.
When I looked back, I was driving a red,
top-down Mercedes, with Kathy by my side.

We hurtled along sun-drenched avenues,
up towards Kathy's hillside mansion
where there would be a Barbie-shaped pool,
Labradoodles serving drinks in bow ties,
and a never-ending supply of fluffy pink fairy cakes,
but I had no idea how I knew all that.

The Magician

The barber held up a mirror
and showed me the back of my head.
I hate it, I said, *What about his?*
Nodding towards the twenty-something-
year-old skin-head
slouched in the next chair.
The barber shuffled towards him
and held up the mirror.
It's not bad, I said, *a little aggressive,
but not bad. What about his?*
Pointing towards the middle-aged man
with the pink Mohican.
The barber shrugged; lurched towards him,
raised the mirror.
I like it, I said, *I'll take that one.*
An excellent choice, said the barber,
wrapping the mirror in green gift paper
then placing it gently inside a plastic bag.
You won't be disappointed, he said.
At home, I carefully unwrapped the mirror
then hung it above the fireplace.
When I stepped back,

the Mohawk-man's head was gone.
Amazing, I thought, *it's like magic...*
Like REAL magic...
I poured myself a glass of wine
and reclined on the sofa, not feeling
disappointed at all.

Future Appliances

Spiderwebs hung from the washing line.
Autumn crept into my bones like small cell carcinoma.
I consulted with a bottle of red.
It said everything would come up petals
and sprig leaves before the spring
but added mysteriously that I should avoid flying
for at least the next seventeen years.
I blustered through a poem about love gone wrong
but wondered if the bottle of red
knew more than it was telling.
I visited the washing machine
who reassured me that life is much like a long-spin cycle
but advised I avoid archery or wild swimming
for the next nineteen weeks, or until the dark clouds
it saw swirling above my head had dissipated.
That's when the kettle on the worktop whistled me over
and wheezed into my ear that life is nothing
like a long-spin cycle
and is instead like steam evaporating over drab fields
on a winter's day, and that I should avoid any activity
that closely resembles living for at least
the next eighteen months –
and that I should probably just spend it in bed.

That's when the toaster popped up and said,
*No, no, no, you idiot! Life is nothing like a long-spin cycle
or steam evaporating over drab fields on a winter's day.
Life,* he said, *is like a warm piece of toast
that should be smothered in Marmite
then eaten immediately before it gets cold.
Leave only the crumbs for the mice
and the plate for the dishwasher.*
I lay down on the cold kitchen tiles
and cupped my hands over my ears
while the small appliances argued amongst themselves.
You can't take it with you! Rattled the dishwasher.
Once you're gone, you're gone, said the toaster.
Which was probably for the best, I thought.

Scarecrow

'Oh joy! Rapture! I've got a brain!' – The Scarecrow, The Wizard of Oz.

Dorothy, Dotty, Doll, Big D
whatever it is you like to be called these days
when you left me here
to the town drunks
and the mice
and deep time
with a traffic cone for a hat
and an idiot's brain,
Bitch,
I thought I might die.
Thought I might go mad
from all this thinking.
But this morning,
as the sun cracked
like an egg
beyond the sycamore trees
my brain sketched a new image of you -
Older now, sixty-pounds heavier
waiting on tables in some greasy bar,
three kids at home,
boyfriend in prison,
five-digit-credit-card-debt.

Then later,
locked inside a bathroom stall
tears streaking down your cheeks.
Clicking your heels as fast as you can
but going nowhere.

You're Welcome

On the fourth day
of the rest of your life

you are arguing the case
for neoclassicism

in the age of Meta
wearing a wound

the size of Nepal
on your forehead.

You are quite sane,
YES, you are quite

sane, as you point
the laser pen

towards the PowerPoint
presentation

of pink flamingos bathing
in the tepid waters

of Sub-Saharan Africa.
Occasionally,

a passer-by stops
and glances up

from their shopping trolley
to ask if you're okay?

and you say, *yes*
YES, I am perfectly opaque.

But the blood? They say.
It's nothing, a scratch,

you reassure them.
Notice the stance, you say,

gesturing towards the next slide.
Pink but heroically poised.

Homeresque in its nature
with a hint of Marilyn.

It's a pink flamingo,
someone says.

Yes, you say,
what else do you see?

Some birds, the sky,
the tumbling branches...

Exactly, you say.
But isn't this the help desk? They say.

You're welcome, you say.

Dr. Freud

Alan was sandwiched between shelving units
in the wine and spirits section of ALDI's supermarket.
Everything alright, Alan? I asked,
peering through cut-price whiskeys
and the cheapest of merlots.
Keep your voice down, Alan said,
I'm having that dream again.
What dream? I asked.
*You know...the dream where I'm shopping in ALDI's,
I look down and discover I'm completely naked.*
But Alan, I said, *it's four o'clock on a Tuesday afternoon,
you can't be dreaming.*
Whatever you say, Dr Freud, Alan said.
I'll go home and get you some clothes. I said.
No, he said, *I'll be waking up any moment now.*
Let me call your wife, I said.
You don't understand, Alan said,
*I have the same dream every day until precisely 4.04pm.
Then I wake up, back in the real world.*
But, Alan, I said, *this* is *the real world.*
You always say that, Alan said.
*Just wait, I'll be waking up anytime now,
and then you'll see.*

I looked into Alan's feral eyes
until his wild gaze became unbearable.
I turned away to slip a bottle of Jameson's
beneath my jacket.
When I looked back,
Alan was gone.

The Letter

When my wife receives a letter
from the Digital Surveillance Clinic,

I wonder if she is secretly working for the Government.

Spooling information about our whereabouts
back to HQ like the sleepy apps that doze on my phone.

But I discover it's a letter from the local opticians,
whose recent change of name confuses itself with an elite
counter-terrorist unit.

And for the rest of the morning, I'm imagining Derek,
Fifty-two years old.

Single. Alone in his mother's house.

A sly grin the size of cheddar gorge, spliced
across his pitted face

as he smugly updates his dating profile

from occupation – *Optician*
to occupation – *Digital Surveillance Analyst*.

Eagerly anticipating the tsunami of fanny,
he'll soon be steeped in.

Hi, I'm Derek, Digital Surveillance Analyst,
I like fast cars and expensive cheeses.

Hi, I'm Derek, Digital Surveillance Analyst,
I like mixed martial arts and wakeboarding.

No more jokes about not having been to spec savers.
No more visually challenged dates seeking free eye tests.

No more future Father-In-Laws flexing
dagger tattoos aggressively across crowded bars.

Now that Derek's been promoted
he is supercharged, confident,

sauntering through life on some invisible force.

Cutting up drivers in his Renault Clio.
Complaining in restaurants
about meals he previously enjoyed.

With a simple change of job title,
Derek's world has transformed
into something pulsing, something alive.

Something vital.

I think of my own job title –
Idiot

And consider a change to *Digital Imbecile*
or *Strategic Nincompoop*

but can't decide between the two

so resign myself to the half-life
of idiot
for the foreseeable future.

Colony

The mind lurches like a drunk towards oblivion.
You must work for the Colony, they say,
you must contribute.

You must give your heart,
your soul, your brains, your balls
you must pay your taxes

for three small meals a day,
a little wine,

some cigarettes
and a room you will never own
and then

you will die.

The other ants cheer;
Dumb little fuckers
happy little fuckers

whistling merrily
towards the grave.

Dumber

For Christmas, I wanted a gift
that would make me even dumber than I already was.
So I visited PC World
for advice on lowering my intelligence levels
to the thickest humanly possible
whilst continuing to function
as a semi-valuable member of society.
The shop assistant, Phil,
nodded knowingly
and said he had just the device for me.
He led me to a large mobile phone rack
and pointed towards the new iPhone 98
which he told me could filter out
all reliable news sources
and replace them entirely with conspiracy theories
and fake social media accounts.
It's a great bit of kit, I said, *but I already have one,*
and whilst it's dumbed me down significantly,
I am still acutely aware of my environment
and conversations taking place in my vicinity,
which I find unbearably painful.
Phil slapped me on my back
and beamed his inhumanly white teeth.

I've got just the thing!
I followed him through to the IPad department
where he explained that the newest fifty-inch model
could be connected to my brain
where it could read, think and even speak for me.
I could sleep twenty-four hours of the day
oblivious to the world around me
and no one would be any the wiser,
least of all me.
Bag it up, I said to Phil.
This is exactly what I've been looking for.
I was excited to try out the new device,
so on Christmas day morning,
after opening presents with my wife
I switched the device on and fell asleep until late May.
When I woke, I was standing on a beach;
the tepid ocean foaming around my toes.
I love it when you quote, Heidegger, my wife said.
*Tell me more about the metaphysical evolution
of the original sin, my darling.*
I tried to speak, but nothing came out.
A rivulet of spittle dribbled from the corner of my mouth.
NOM-NOM, I said.
Yes, it really is perfect, isn't it? My wife said,
gazing at the blood-orange sun
beginning to sink behind the waves.

Yes, I thought, *I suppose it is,* switching the machine on
and dissolving back into dreamless,
bottomless
sleep.

Statues

I tried to reason with Martin –
tried to show him the error of his ways –
but Martin wouldn't back down.
It's free speech gone nuts, he protested.
The statues in Martin's living room
eyeballed us suspiciously from their pedestals.
Of course, Idi Amin made mistakes, Martin said,
but does that give us the right to toss his statue into the Thames?
Yes, Martin, I said. *It really does.*
Bollocks, Martin said. *It's history!*
Please, Martin, his wife said,
they're threatening to burn down the house.
A giant bronze Pinochet smirked at us
from behind the coffee table.
Martin, I said. *These men and women
killed lots and lots of people
and did very bad things; we shouldn't be celebrating them.*
A brick exploded through the window
and landed in the lap of Benito Mussolini.
Please, Martin. It's not too late, I said.
Martin began to cry.

I just thought they made the living room look nice, Martin said. *I know,* I said, pulling Martin in for a bearhug, *we all did, but now it's time to let them go.*

A Discourse In Cultural Heritage

The white seagulls chased the black crows
around the cloudless sky.

The black crows chased the white seagulls
around the cloudless sky.

You will respect our cultural heritage,
Squawked the white seagulls to the black crows.

No, you will respect OUR cultural heritage,
Squawked the black crows to the white seagulls

and this went on for several centuries
until the white seagulls
had forgotten all about their cultural heritage

and the black crows had forgotten
all about their cultural heritage

and when the white seagulls and the black crows
had collectively forgotten all about their cultural heritage

they squabbled over who owned the cloudless sky.

In This Game We Are Playing

At the party,
we write down abstract nouns
to describe how we are feeling.
Words like happy,
sad, anxious,
content.
Then, fix them to our foreheads
like post-it-sized howls for help.
I write *The Hillsborough Disaster*
and fasten it to my skull
like an inoperable tumour
because I want to express
that I feel suffocated,
hemmed-in,
unable to exhale in modern society.
Jaredd-With-The-Two-D's
and wearing the word *Tolerant*
says he finds my label
grotesquely offensive –
which,
I suppose,
is the point I am trying to make.

Apology

All day, I sidle around the rooms of my house
apologising for my existence.

To the open packet of chilli Doritos
on the kitchen worktop
I apologise for my insatiable need to consume.

To the TV in the living room, I say,
I'm sorry that I have used you like a wayward
oracle to form my slanted view of the world.

To the fish-slicer slouched in the kitchen drawer,
I say, I'm sorry for not involving you more often
in my vanilla sex life.

To the endless shelves of CDs stacked in the hall, I say,
I'm sorry that advancements in technology
have forced me to abandon you.

To the landscape painting slung on the bedroom wall,
I say, I'm sorry for not believing in a land
where nature flourishes all year round.

To my scant collection of feminist literature
buried deep inside my wardrobe, I say,
I'm sorry for being straight, white and male.

To the footstool slumped in the living room,
I say, I'm sorry, that for too long
I have let my feet rest upon you like two dead fish
on the surface of a frozen pond.

To the open packet of Fluoxetine in the bathroom cabinet,
I say, I'm sorry, you could not make me happier.

To the piles and piles of unpublished poems,
I apologise for being a talentless, fuck-face-hack
who had no right to believe that words
might ever sing for me.

Then I pack my suitcase as if I'm going on a journey.
But the only place I am going

is to a land where night follows night

and existence is a prayer whispered from the shadows
that I cannot hear

> because I'm dead,
> *silly*.

Tattoo

For my fortieth birthday
I had a loaf of bread
tattooed above my left bicep
to honour the Natufian tribe
who were the first to harvest
grains for bread.

Next, I had the tattooist
carve the image
of a Beef & Tomato flavoured
Pot Noodle
across my collar bone
to represent consumerism
in the modern age.

Finally, she etched
a blue beard on my face -
one I could be buried in
and that wouldn't shave off
or grow grey with age.

In the next chair
I could hear a woman
requesting the names and birthdates
of all four members of *Bauhaus*
stamped across her breasts.

Goths, I said to the tattooist,
What are they like, eh?

Return To Babel

What language will they speak in heaven?
Is a question I am contemplating this morning
as the daytime moon lurches
high above the heads of the living.

Because there are so many languages in the world.
And what if everyone speaks Latin or Greek
or worse,   Welsh?

How will I make them understand
that the words I have spoken
weren't always the thoughts I was thinking?

How will I convey
that even in the late Jurassic epoch of my thirties,
I was still growing. Learning
not to be an arsehole?

How will I say that for most of my life
I have kept myself away from others.
Not through selfishness or arrogance

but through fear of causing harm to others
or of others causing harm to me?

Will I need to mime in that awkward
Englishman-abroad way
to explain my reasons for not having children of my own?

Cheeks puffed out,
lips pursed,
hands expanding

as I make the sound of the atom bomb.

Postcoital

We should swallow the lot
and be done with it, Marsha says,

as I play the sad piano like it's 1954.
Plinkerty-plink, plinkerty-

plunk, all painted lips and gooey, red eyes.
A fly crawls in and out of our mouths.

Plaster tumbles from the ceiling -
paints our greasy hair.

We lost the plot after season five
over fishing rights and the free movement of people.

Imagine a map without edges, Marsha says,

Imagine...

I get so anxious now even my toes ache.
Lately, I've been seeing God
everywhere.

TV Made Us Fat But Look At Us Now

When I hurtled
like a comet
from that small town
known as *The Past*
and zoomed
head first
into its neighbouring city,
The Present,
I had no idea
there would be so few
humans here.
Just sedated
avatars
who looked like humans
but weren't humans,
operated remotely
from a planet
called *The Internet* -
And when I looked
at their sleepy faces,
their pallid skin
and their ridiculous
choice in world leaders,

I wanted to build a bridge
or a road
or a superhighway
back into the small town
known as *The Past*.
But time travel
had not been invented.
And who in their present
state of mind
would have the energy
to build a bridge
or a road
or a superhighway
large enough to span
the mechanics
of space
and time
or lay anything down
for the benefit of mankind,
when there was so much
to watch on TV?

Horseplay

I was sitting in a field
        watching the mottled clouds
 make angry faces

                when a man in a grey hoodie
            whistled me over to the fence and said,

Alright, mate,
wanna buy this brand new
        definitely NOT
          stolen
     mobile phone?

It's a phone, I said, *what would I want with a phone?*
I'm a horse.

                You're not a horse, he said.

Yes I am, I said, *I've been a horse in these fields*
            for forty-four years.

Well I've never seen you before, said the man,
and you don't look like a horse to me.

Look, I said,
can you get me out of here?

Why don't you jump the fence? He asked.

*I'm an old horse
with old knees,* I said.

If you owned this phone, he said, *you could call for help.*

I'm a horse, I said,
I don't have any fingers.

It's your loss, pal, said the man,
you won't get a phone cheaper than this.

I could be your horse, I said,
*you could ride me through the streets
selling stolen phones to the poor
like a pound-shop, Robin Hood.*

I'm allergic to horses, he said and sneezed.

Piss off then before I call the police, I said.

You're a horse; you don't have a phone, he said.

Just then, my wife appeared in the field
carrying fresh water and dry kibble

making a sort of clicking noise with her tongue
and trilling in a high, sing-songy voice,

Come on boy! Come and get your dinner, John...
Who's been a good boy for mummy then?

Please, I said to the hooded man, *We don't have much time...*
You have to get me out of here.

Proper Gangsta

The
dog
bit
the
post
man
so
we
had
him
de-
stroyed.
The
dog
is
doing
quite
well.

Vaba Banga

A mystic of sorts;
he reads people's arseholes.
Sniffs out bad omens.
Predicts future catastrophes.
It's dirty work, the mystic says,
tracing the lifeline of the King's
wrinkled sphincter.
But without foreknowledge,
this Kingdom would have fallen
to the treacherous Scots
and revolting Republicans,
decades ago.
Quite right, the King says.
I foresee a time of peace approaching, Sire,
the Mystic says,
peering into the great cavern
of the King's hairy rectum.
Good, says the King.
It will last for three days and three nights,
says the Mystic.
And then much death and bloodshed
shall rain from the sky.

Excellent, says the King.
Should we prepare the victory feast?
The Mystic frowns.
To be certain of victory, Sire,
I will need to read the arseholes
of all three princesses, Cilla the handmaiden,
and your loyal dog, Duke.
Of course, says the King.
I will also need to make love to The Queen
several times a day.
I wouldn't expect anything less, says The King.
After all, the fate of our fair Kingdom
rests entirely on your mad,
but occasionally accurate rantings.

Spiritualist Night At The Old Bull Inn

The psychic medium
bathed in majestic blue light,
with the scouse accent
and the native American spirit guide
named, Grey Wolf,
tells us that Terry has returned;

Leave-voting-Terry,
who now carries forth
a message of love and unity
and the urgency of waste recycling
in the post Brexit age.

'Recycle!' Terry is telling us
through the medium of Grey Wolf
'Separate your plastics from your food waste
and always wash your tin cans.'

Speaks the man whose kitchen
was once as familiar to him as the back streets
of Benghazi.

Planet Woman

On planet Woman
every man's penis
is chained to his testicles.

Erections are impossible –
or at least –
painful,   sometimes
fatal.

The women tease us with their nakedness.

Make us apologise
to the towering statue
of Sylvia Plath.

We are sorry Ted Hughes was a flawed but talented bastard.
We are sorry Ted Hughes was a flawed but talented bastard.
We are sorry Ted Hughes was a flawed but talented bastard.

Not all men are the same,
we mutter under our febrile breaths.
Though we know this too, is a lie.

Strange Fish

On Wednesdays,
I carry an atlas to the pub

and unfold it on the cherry-wood bar
and say, *Look,*

look how small we all are
and how big the ocean is.

Look, I say, placing my pint glass
over the jigsaw piece of England,

look, how we all fit
beneath the bottom of a beer glass
like particles of ash.

Look, I say,
shouldn't we learn to love each other more?

You're a strange fish, alright, says the Landlord,
bending down to knuckle

the matted fur
of his invisible French Terrier.

A Musical Theatre Piece Based On The Story Of The Windrush Generation And Played Exclusively By White, Upper-Class Actors

Wasn't the most considered work of art to be performed at the local village hall.

But then neither was Tracey Emin's, *Bed*,
and who didn't want to sleep in that?

Yellow Submarine

When I hear The Beatles,
Yellow Submarine
playing on the radio.
I want to ask Paul McCartney,
how many is *We*?
As in – *'We all live in a yellow submarine'*.
Because submarines are notoriously pokey.
And who exactly are the *We*?
And does the aforementioned
Yellow Submarine
allow for small pets, druids
and humans on housing benefits?
Or is the '*We*' referring only
to John, Paul, Ringo and George?
And what of the mean-spirited, LeRoi Jones,
who accused the song of being a reflection
of White American exclusivity?
Didn't he realize that the Beatles were British?
And that John was a vocal advocate for equality.
And does everything *really* have to be boiled down
to race, colour and creed, Leroi?
Why can't there be a submarine

where the 'We' might live happily together
regardless of gender, race and colour?
Because that, Leroi Jones,
would surely be a submarine
worth singing about.

Jackpot

In May, rain punctures the grass.
The sun struggles to eclipse
the milky clouds.
On TV, a couple basks in the nuclear glow
of having won the world's largest lottery jackpot.
I watch their bulbous faces beamed
into my living room
as they contemplate the ramifications
of having too much money to spend in a lifetime.
They talk of quitting jobs.
Buying a house in the Bahamas.
Hiring the *Arctic Monkeys*
to play *AM* at their wedding.
And I wonder why I should even give a fuck?
Dreams do come true, the TV insists.
So keep paying your taxes.
Keep working your pathetic jobs.
Keep starving on food-bank-hand-me-outs.
But do it with a Nationalist song in your heart.
Knowing that someone out there – just like you –
is now richer than the small country of Somalia.
Tomorrow the news will return to the war in Ukraine
and the cost-of-living crisis. But for now,

I watch this strange juxtaposition
of two people who look like me
and sound like me
but are definitely not me,
cracking open bottles of champagne,
dancing beneath a shower of bubbles,
as if it was money raining from the sky.

Every Crack Represents A Life I Have Saved

- *Dennis Hopper on the set of 'Apocalypse Now.'*

In drama therapy,
I am playing the part of Dennis Hopper
on the set of *Apocalypse Now*.
I'm three days into a ten-day bender;
unshaven, bug-eyed, spouting
LSD monologues about my ex-girlfriend.
My Therapist, playing Brando,
wants to know why I'm such a selfish prick?
Why I can't stop drinking?
How do I *really* feel about my father?
My last two rizlas are tear-soddened;
Soaked.
Brando tells me to sculpt myself into a shape
that best represents how I feel.
I fall to the floor,
scrunch my head between my knees,
curl into a tight ball;
stay there.
Until the noise screeching
up from my lungs

cracks,
frightens us both.

The Drill

A drill is drilling through the neighborhood.
It drills through the morning.
It drills through the afternoon.
It drills through late summer evenings.
We search for the drill.
We follow the sound of its drilling
through streets, through fields,
through rickety church yards.
We say, what can a drill be drilling
at all hours of the day?
We say, I can't hear you over the sound
of the drilling. SPEAK UP!
The drill keeps drilling.
Coffee cups ratchet across the kitchen table.
Picture frames tumble from the walls.
We shout, *we can't go on with this damn drilling!*
The drill keeps drilling.
It drills into our skulls.
It drills through our pincered lives.
We say, *why is the drill still drilling?*
When will the drilling stop? We say, *SPEAK UP!*
For God's sake, PLEASE,
SPEAK UP!

The Dream Shop

I was tortured by my dreams
so I visited the dream shop
to exchange them for less frightening dreams.
I was particularly interested in sex dreams
or flying dreams
or dreams about chocolate fountains
I explained to the shop assistant,
who was floating lotus-style
above a rack of miscellaneous dreams.
Please, he hissed,
hauling me by my jacket towards the checkout.
They'll hear you!
Who? I asked, looking around the empty store.
The dreams, he said. *We don't judge or label here, Pal.*
One person's nightmare is another person's wet dream.
We let the dreams decide which they'd prefer to identify with.
Makes sense, I said.
Do you have any dreams who identify with flying dreams
or sex dreams?
For Christ's sake! The shop assistant barked.
What is it now? I asked.
We don't deadname here, fella. I think you should leave.
Please, I said, *I'm desperate.*

I only dream of visiting dream shops
whose shop assistants find the dreams I want to buy
extremely offensive.
Sounds like a nightmare, said the shop assistant.
It is, I said, *it really is...*
I can't help you, he said. *Have you tried the shop next door?*
Yes, I said, *many, many times.*

A Message To Future Cat Generations

The cat sleeps curled at his desk
while I punch at keys late into the afternoon.

He would like me to get his thoughts down here.
He would like to commit them to metrical form
so that all future cat generations

might avoid the catastrophic fuck-ups
we humans made.

But he sleeps mostly
or twitches wildly in mid-dream
which means he is not thinking of anything;

A zen-like metaphor,

I am trying to put
into words.

A Zero-Tolerance Approach

I was drinking bottles of Peroni
and attacking a triangle-shaped
cheese and onion sandwich
by a blazing log fire at The Bull Inn
when the local drug dealer, Claude,
crawled beneath the table and bit my shin.
What the fuck, Claude? I said,
as blood pumped from the wound
like an uncorked bottle of champagne.
Bravo! Mike, the Landlord roared from behind the bar.
Claude rose to his knees and barked like a dog.
I'm bleeding, I said. *It hurts...*
Claude is very thorough, Mike said.
I don't understand, I said.
Claude is our new sniffer dog, Mike said proudly.
*The Brewery has demanded a zero-tolerance approach
to drug problems on the premises,
and Claude seemed like the obvious candidate to help.*
But Claude IS the Bull Inn's drug problem, I said.
Exactly, Mike said. *It's win-win for everyone.*
I went back to eating my cheese and onion sandwich
until Trevor, the local professional wrestler,

picked me up and body-slammed me
into the waste recycling bin.
What the fuck, Trevor? I said.
Trevor grunted and walked back to the bar.
And I suppose Trevor's the new cleaner? I said to Mike.
No, Mike said, *that's just Trevor being Trevor.*

Buddha On A Bicycle.

When Claude turns forty
he buys a pair of spandex
shorts, blue aviator shades,
a pink water bottle
and attacks hills on his bicycle
like he's fifteen again.
Claude snaps photos of himself -
Sweat covered,
gurning, silhouetting sunsets
on snowy peaks.
He posts them on Instagram
with motivational quotes like –
Don't stop until your chain falls off!
Never give up!
Brakes are for pussies!
Claude is cycling for his life.
Claude is cycling from his life.
Claude is cycling towards certain death.
He just doesn't know it yet.
Claude is zen-zen on his bicycle.
Claude has clarity of thought
like a bony Buddha on a bicycle
as he reconnects with his masculinity

his drive for accomplishment
and a desire for minor victories
that he can share with his children
and his grandchildren
and that someday
will be retold in a 2x1cm
obituary in the local newspaper.
Meanwhile, Claude's wife
sleeps with anyone
who isn't Claude.

Discombobulation

What time

    will our minds

        be home for tea?

I ask my wife, who is combing her hair
with the goldfish bowl.

It is already late,
and most of us haven't seen our minds in weeks.

We watch a lost herd of minds trek aimlessly
across the Chinese peninsula, live on TV.

No one knows where our minds are going,
A sad voiceover says. *But some of us want them back.*

On the next channel, a news reporter interviews
an old man who lost his mind months ago -

*Is it right that a man without a mind
should be running the country?*
The interviewer asks.

WOOF!, says the President.

And since we've all lost our minds, anyway
we couldn't agree with him more.

An Existential Crisis

Lately, I have become so withdrawn
I have hired a machine to have conversations
with the dishwasher.

I don't want to explain myself to modern appliances.

Do dishwashers have souls? The Machine asks.
Of course not, I say, machines don't have souls.

Then why is the dishwasher screaming? The machine asks.
Because machines don't have souls, I say.

The machine screams.

Why are you screaming? I ask the machine.
Because I don't have a soul, the Machine says.

I scream.
The dishwasher screams.
The Machine screams.

Why are we screaming? We scream.

But nobody hears us above the sound of our screaming.

The Art Gallery

I opened an art gallery in my head
and filled its walls with empty canvases.

Nobody came except for the blind man
and his golden retriever,
who had mistaken me for the CO-OP next door.

I pressed a long-handled paintbrush
into the folds of his fingers.

Show me, I said, guiding his hand gently
towards the canvas.

> *He painted*
> *long and slow*
> *in large*
> *swirling loops --*
> *a monstrous shadow.*

Then later,
at home, presumably –
a slanderous review.

Procession

I know what you're thinking;

Why wait limply in line
when you could feign disability
and be carried languidly like a Roman
deity to the front of the queue?

I am always admonishing myself.

In America, veterans stand at events
to be applauded by unspoilt,
unbloodied hands.

I am not a veteran.
But I stand because I like the applause.
What's wrong with that?

If you can clap for those who have bisected
the bones of beings
with bullets and bombs,

surely you can clap for me?

Who has never injured anyone,
or achieved much in life,
honestly.

Post Historic Shame.

My friends say I'm wasteful.
I purchased a life that I do not use.

The mechanism scares me.

My past life regression therapist
claims I was the bomb that destroyed Hiroshima.

She refuses to work with me on serious ethical grounds.

It's what humans made me do, I try to explain.
But she insists,
I am responsible for the deaths of 66,000 souls.

I once met a man who was the reincarnation
of the Birkenau gas chamber.

He rarely spoke and had few friends.

I wanted to tell him it wasn't his fault,
it's what humans made us do.

But my shame was so deep,

I couldn't even look at him.

Blood Axe Books

You want to get published
by *Blood Axe Books*?
He asks.

Then you need to conform.

Write about *FLOWERS* or *FEMINISM*
or *IMMIGRATION*

and use bigger words
like –

INCENDIARY or *INTRAVENOUSLY*.

Infact, try to write
directly from a dictionary

and make sure you use plenty
of *THUS's*.

All the greats used
THUS's!

Shakespeare used thousands of them
and it never did him any harm.

Thus, I took my poems and shoved them intravenously
up his arse.

ACKNOWLEDGEMENTS

Thank you to the editors of *Across The Margin, Apocalypse Confidential, Bear Creek Gazette, Idle Ink, MONO Fiction, Punk Noir Magazine, Outlaw Poetry and Remark Magazine*, where some of these poems first appeared. My sincere thanks to all the presses who have supported my work over the past few decades. I want to thank Mark SaFranko for his invaluable friendship, support and encouragement, without which this collection might never have existed. Thank you to Tom Weir and Joanne Done for their time and generous words. Finally, thank you to Cody Sexton at *Anxiety Press* for bringing this book to publication.

ABOUT THE AUTHOR

Mark Vanner was born in Nottingham in 1978 and now lives in Gloucestershire, UK. He is a writer and artist. His poetry has appeared in numerous anthologies and journals, including Neon, 3am, Ambit, Mono Fiction and many more. For more information, please visit: www.markvanner.com or find him on Twitter: @VannerMark.

Printed in Great Britain
by Amazon